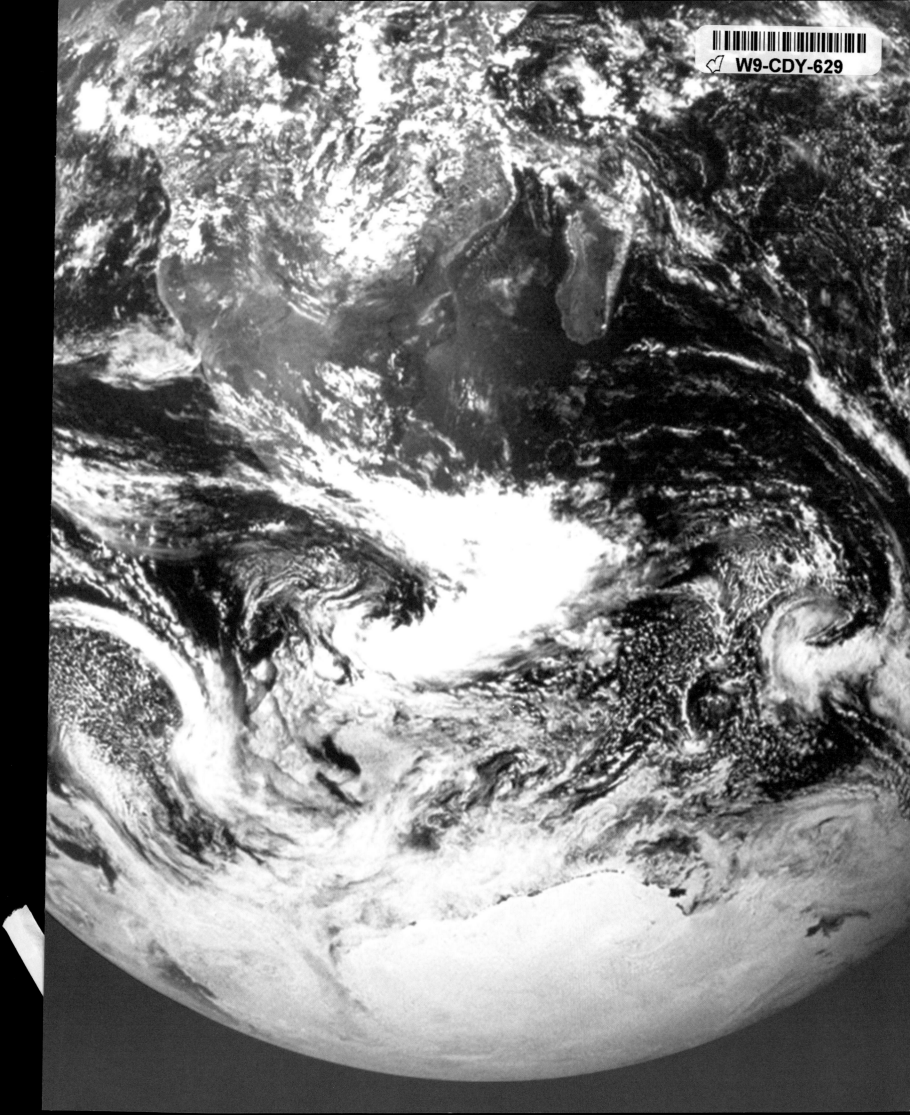

PRIMARY EXPLORERS

SPACE

igloo

Contents

Space is the unknown, too vast to measure, full of mysteries. Explorers on Earth have been everywhere on land. Only space and Earth's ocean depths, remain unexplored.

The Astronomer (1668), a painting by the Dutch artist, Johannes Vermeer.

Astronomers have gazed at the Sun, Moon and stars since ancient times. Many ancient people believed the stars and planets shaped life and events on Earth.

Telescopes changed our view of space and the universe in which we live.

A copy of Isaac Newton's reflecting telescope of the 1600s.

WHY IS SPACE SO EXCITING?

Space is not empty, as the name suggests. There are billions of other planets to be explored.

People dreamed of spaceflight long before they had the technology to make it possible.

NOT ALONE IN THE UNIVERSE?

In ancient times, people believed the sky was the home of gods. Most people believed that the Sun revolved around Earth. Copernicus, a Polish scientist of the 1500s, changed this view. He shocked many people by saying that scientific observation showed that Earth moved around the Sun. We now know the Sun is just one of billions of stars. Other stars could have Earth-like planets orbiting them, and they could contain life-forms, too.

People observed the movements of the Sun and Moon to make calendars. They gave names to the star-patterns in the night sky – the constellations. Some people built special observatories, such as Stonehenge in England, to study the movement of the stars, which they believed had an important influence on their daily lives. Ceremonies were held when the stars reached certain positions in the sky.

Stonehenge, England

In the 1960s, people were thrilled to watch the first Apollo Moon landings on TV. Every spaceflight in the 1950s and 1960s made headline news and seemed quite incredible. Today, we take spaceflight almost for granted. But it is still exciting to see a rocket launch into space, or images of an astronaut drifting far above our beautiful blue-green planet. Some people have already experienced the wonders of space for themselves, as space tourists, and this is a rapidly developing industry.

Astronauts in space get a breathtaking view of our world. We can share the magic through TV and the internet, following each mission as it unfolds.

EARTH AND ITS MOON

Earth is the third planet from the Sun. It has one natural satellite, the Moon.

Earth began as a cloud of dust grains. Gravity squashed the cloud into a hot, dense ball – it heated up as it was squashed, and this released the gases that became Earth's atmosphere. As the ball cooled, a hard rock crust formed.

EARTH FROM SPACE

Seen from space, Earth is a blue and white ball (oceans and clouds), with patches of brown and green (land masses). It is slightly flattened at the north and south poles. It also bulges at the middle, the Equator.

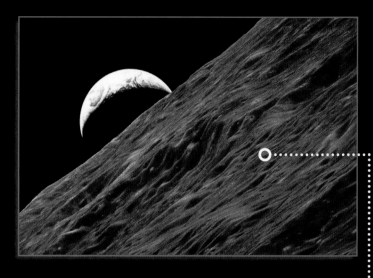

If you were on the Moon (in the foreground), you would see Earth in the sky just as we see the Moon in the sky. Earth in this case appears crescent-shaped because the Sun is shining from the side.

Earth from space is revealed in all its beauty by space cameras.

DID YOU KNOW?

In ancient times, many people associated the Moon with birth and death because it seemed to grow and then die (shrink and disappear). They believed it was a goddess.

| Waxing crescent | Full Moon | Waning crescent | New Moon |

The changes in shape of the Moon are called its phases. They are caused by the Sun shining on different sides of it, as it orbits Earth. The waxing phases are when it is growing and the waning phases are when it is shrinking.

CIRCLING EARTH

Whatever the phase of the Moon, we always see the same side. This is because the Moon turns once on its axis in exactly the same time it takes to circle Earth – every 29½ days. The phase we see depends on the position of the Moon in its orbit around Earth.

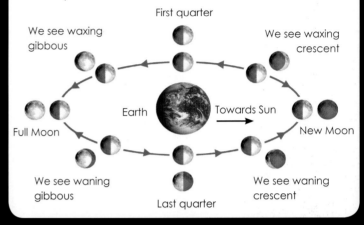

First quarter

We see waxing gibbous

We see waxing crescent

Earth

Towards Sun

Full Moon

New Moon

We see waning gibbous

We see waning crescent

Last quarter

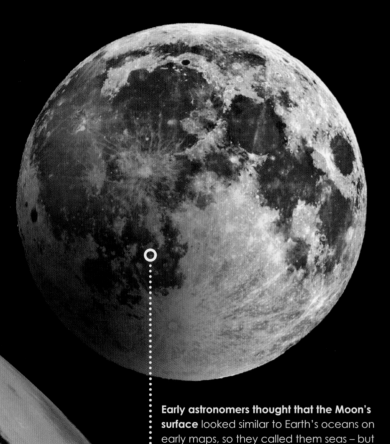

Early astronomers thought that the Moon's surface looked similar to Earth's oceans on early maps, so they called them seas – but there is no surface water on the Moon, and no air either.

Lunar craters are formed by meteoroids and asteroids crashing into the Moon. This crater, called Daedalus, was seen from *Apollo 11* in 1969.

THE MOON'S SURFACE

The Moon's rugged surface is covered in rocky mountains and dusty plains. The highest mountains rise about as high as the highest peaks on Earth. The plains were the safest landing sites for the first lunar astronauts, although they are pitted with thousands of craters – some about 140 miles (225 km) across.

ROCKET FIRSTS

1942 Germany launches the first rocket able to fly high enough to get into space – a V-2 (the first long-range ballistic missile).

Oct 4, 1957 The Soviet Union's Vostok R-7 rocket (based on an ICBM, or intercontinental ballistic missile) launches the world's first satellite, placing Sputnik 1 into a low Earth orbit.

Nov 3, 1957 The Soviet Union launches Sputnik 2 using the Vostok rocket.

Dec 6, 1957 America's Vanguard rocket (built to launch the first US satellite) explodes on the launch pad, on live television.

1958 The US rocket Juno 1 (a four-stage rocket) launches America's first satellite, Explorer 1.

1958 America's first successful Vanguard launching.

1961 A Soviet Vostok rocket puts the first cosmonaut into Earth-orbit.

1969 America's giant Saturn 5 rocket sends Apollo astronauts to the Moon.

1973 Europe develops the expendable (to be used only once) Ariane rocket.

1999 Europe's Ariane 5 is successfully launched.

2010 Chinese space scientists plan to build a Moon-rocket the size of Saturn 5.

ROCKETS INTO SPACE

Rockets can send spacecraft into orbit around the Earth and far beyond, to explore outer space.

The first rockets were firework rockets, made in China about 1,000 years ago. By the 1950s, scientists had made liquid-fuel rockets powerful enough to escape Earth's gravity and travel into space.

ROCKET SCIENCE
A rocket has a propulsion system (engines and fuel) and a guidance system (steering). Most rockets have two, or three parts, or stages, one on top of the other. Boosters give extra power for lift-off. Only the top stage carrying the spacecraft (the payload) goes into space.

Robert H. Goddard tested this liquid-fuel rocket in 1926. It burned a mixture of petrol and oxygen.

Vanguard launched America's second Earth satellite in 1958. Vanguard was a small rocket built for science research.

FIRST ROCKETS INTO SPACE
Both Soviet Union and America used German V-2 rockets to develop space rockets in the 1940s. Soviet Union Vostok rocket launched the world's first cosmonaut, Yuri Gagarin, in 1961. Vostok was bigger than any American rocket, until Saturn 5, measuring 111 m (363 ft) tall, was launched in the 1960s. Later, France and Japan built their own rockets to launch satellites, followed by China, Britain and India.

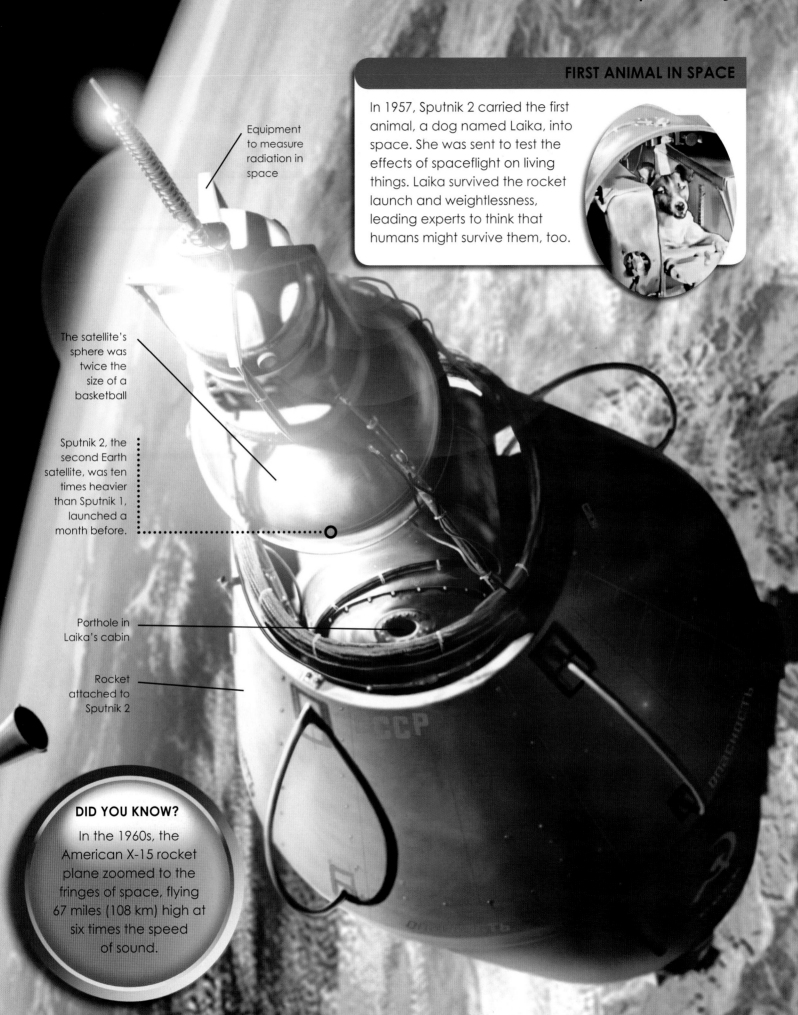

Equipment to measure radiation in space

FIRST ANIMAL IN SPACE

In 1957, Sputnik 2 carried the first animal, a dog named Laika, into space. She was sent to test the effects of spaceflight on living things. Laika survived the rocket launch and weightlessness, leading experts to think that humans might survive them, too.

The satellite's sphere was twice the size of a basketball

Sputnik 2, the second Earth satellite, was ten times heavier than Sputnik 1, launched a month before.

Porthole in Laika's cabin

Rocket attached to Sputnik 2

DID YOU KNOW?

In the 1960s, the American X-15 rocket plane zoomed to the fringes of space, flying 67 miles (108 km) high at six times the speed of sound.

SATELLITES AND WHAT THEY DO

Artificial satellites orbit Earth and send back scientific information. They also give us worldwide communications.

A satellite stays in space because it has partly escaped Earth's gravity.
It will stay in orbit until its orbit 'decays' (gets too low). As it re-enters the Earth's atmosphere, it burns up.

SATELLITE LAUNCH SYSTEMS
The biggest satellites are about the size of a car and are packed with scientific instruments. Most satellites are put into space by a rocket-engined ELV (expendable launch vehicle), which is designed to be used only once. A few satellites have been released from Space Shuttles flying around Earth.

Europe's ADM-Aeolus satellite (ADM stands for Atmospheric Dynamics Mission) observes the atmospheric conditions around Earth, especially its wind systems. It is used for weather forecasting and climate research.

SATELLITE FIRSTS

1957 The Soviet Union's Sputnik 1 is the first satellite.

Sputnik 1

1957 Sputnik 2 puts the first animal (Laika) into space.

1958 Explorer 1 is the first US satellite.

1959 Explorer 6 takes the first photos from orbit.

1962 Telstar is the first communications satellite.

1966 The Soviet Union's Luna 10 is the first craft to go into orbit around the Moon.

1968 The US _Apollo 8_ orbits the Moon, but with three astronauts inside.

1971 America's Mariner 9 is the first satellite to orbit Mars and map the red planet.

1975 The Soviet Union's Venera 9 is the first spacecraft to orbit Venus.

1983 The IRAS satellite spots 20,000 new galaxies.

1989 Magellan orbits Venus, mapping most of the planet.

1997 Mars Global Surveyor maps Mars' surface.

2007 Japan's Selene is the biggest spacecraft to visit the Moon since Apollo 17 landed in 1972.

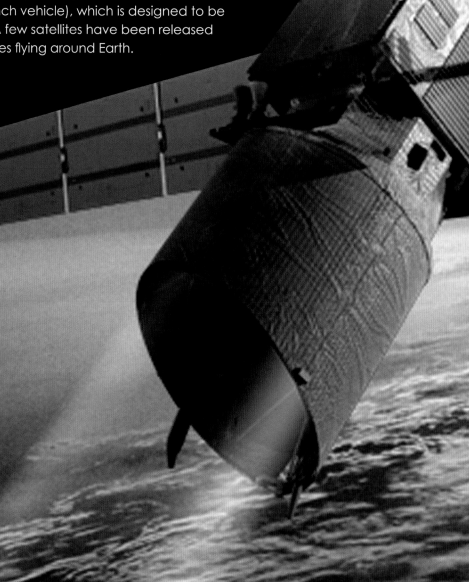

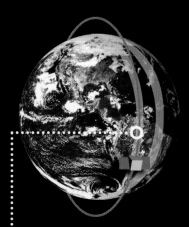

A satellite in a polar orbit passes over the north and south poles and every other bit of Earth's surface at some time, making it ideal for surveying the whole globe.

EARTH SCIENCE SATELLITES

Satellites study changes in the Earth's environment, such as melting ice caps, dwindling forests and spreading deserts. Most satellites get electric power from solar panels fixed to extending 'wings'. The panels convert the Sun's energy into power for the satellite's scientific equipment, computers, cameras and communications systems.

DID YOU KNOW?

The tiny American satellite Vanguard I (1958) was the second US satellite and the first solar-powered satellite. It is the oldest-surviving artificial Earth satellite.

Satellite maps are amazingly accurate. This map was made using data from three satellites. The image shows a view of Pasadena, California in the United States.

WHAT SATELLITES ARE USED FOR

Satellites are used for many purposes. Communication satellites relay telephone and TV signals. Military satellites can spot missile sites and camps. Navigation satellites provide the global positioning system (GPS) used by motorists, pilots and sailors, and there are also weather and science satellites.

Weather satellites, such as NASA's Aqua, spot tropical storms, such as Cyclone Oli.

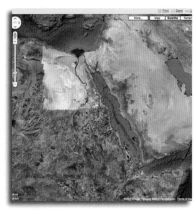

Satellite maps are able to show land use and natural resources in amazing detail.

The GeoEye-1 satellite takes detailed images of Earth, such as this one of the Colosseum in Rome.

EARLY ASTRONAUTS

An astronaut, or cosmonaut in Russia, is someone who travels in space.

The US space agency NASA was set up in 1958, and in 1959 seven US pilots started astronaut training. In the Soviet Union, a similar group was also training for space, among them Yuri Gagarin. Training included brief spells of weightlessness (being without gravity) and tests of physical and mental strength.

SPACE HEROES

Yuri Gagarin flew around the world in 1961 and overnight became a hero. He never flew in space again. Gagarin was followed by other Russian cosmonauts, including in 1963, the first woman in space, Valentina Tereshkova. America's Alan Shepard made a 15-minute space 'hop' in May 1961 and John Glenn was the first American in orbit, in February 1962.

Yuri Gagarin made history on 12 April 1961. His Vostok spacecraft made one orbit of Earth. Gagarin's flight lasted just 108 minutes. He landed by parachute in Russia.

America's Mercury capsule was only 3.5 m (11.5 ft) long, just big enough for one astronaut. Four Mercury flights were made in orbit between February 1962 and May 1963.

John Glenn was one of America's first seven astronauts. He made the first orbital flight by an American in February 1962. In 1998 he flew in a Space Shuttle at the age of 77.

America's Gemini spacecraft carried two astronauts. This is *Gemini 7* seen from *Gemini 6* (December 1965). Russia flew the first three-man craft, *Voskhod 1* (October 1964) and made the first space-walk (March 1965).

SPLASHDOWN!

NASA chose splashdowns to return its first astronauts. After re-entering Earth's atmosphere, spacecraft parachuted down into the sea, where ships were waiting to pick up the crew.

Astronauts Neil Armstrong and David Scott wait in *Gemini 8*. They made an emergency splashdown in March 1966, after the craft encountered problems in space.

DID YOU KNOW?

Astronauts become a little taller in space. Since there is less gravity, their bones are less squashed together. Back on Earth, they return to their normal height.

The first US space-walker was Edward H. White. In his spacesuit, and attached by a safety line, he floated out of *Gemini 4* in June 1965.

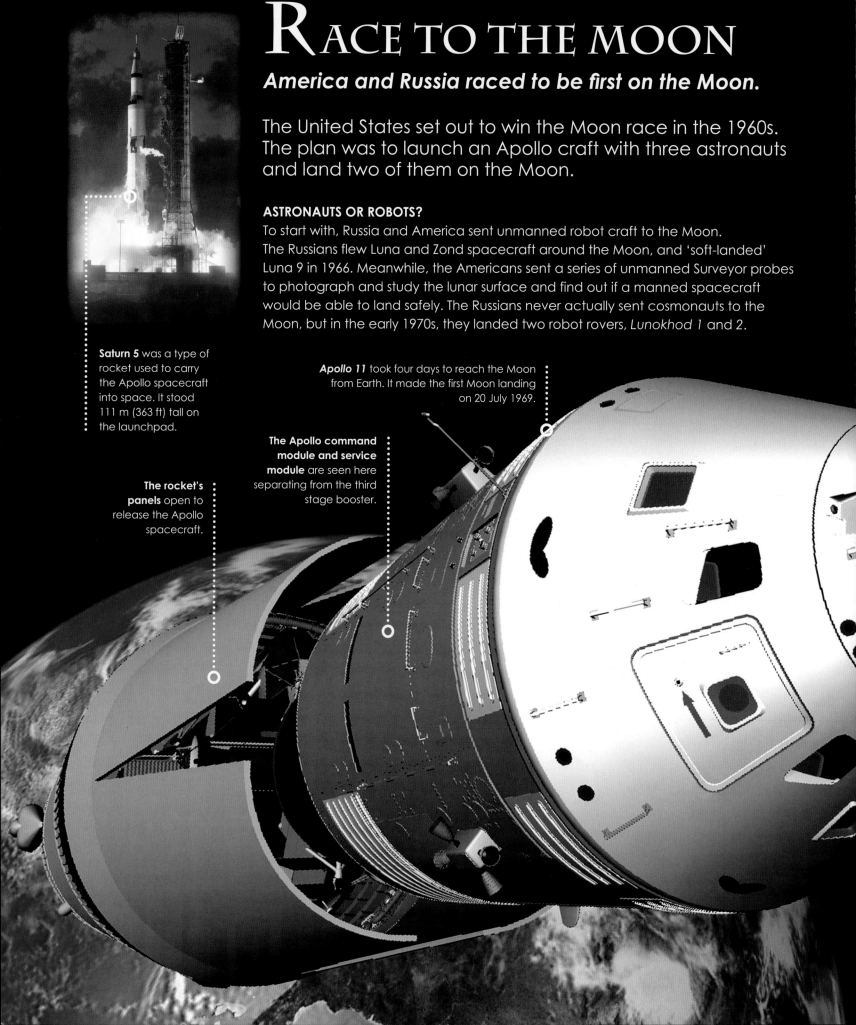

RACE TO THE MOON

America and Russia raced to be first on the Moon.

The United States set out to win the Moon race in the 1960s. The plan was to launch an Apollo craft with three astronauts and land two of them on the Moon.

ASTRONAUTS OR ROBOTS?

To start with, Russia and America sent unmanned robot craft to the Moon. The Russians flew Luna and Zond spacecraft around the Moon, and 'soft-landed' Luna 9 in 1966. Meanwhile, the Americans sent a series of unmanned Surveyor probes to photograph and study the lunar surface and find out if a manned spacecraft would be able to land safely. The Russians never actually sent cosmonauts to the Moon, but in the early 1970s, they landed two robot rovers, *Lunokhod 1* and *2*.

Saturn 5 was a type of rocket used to carry the Apollo spacecraft into space. It stood 111 m (363 ft) tall on the launchpad.

Apollo 11 took four days to reach the Moon from Earth. It made the first Moon landing on 20 July 1969.

The rocket's panels open to release the Apollo spacecraft.

The Apollo command module and service module are seen here separating from the third stage booster.

Luna 3 was the first craft to fly around the Moon (1960) and took the first photos of the far side of the Moon.

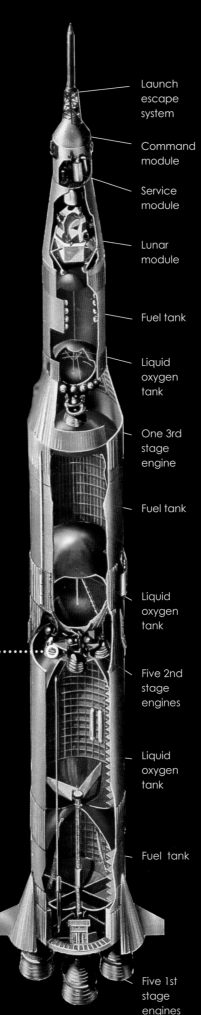

Launch escape system

Command module

Service module

Lunar module

Fuel tank

Liquid oxygen tank

One 3rd stage engine

Fuel tank

Liquid oxygen tank

Five 2nd stage engines

Liquid oxygen tank

Fuel tank

Five 1st stage engines

The Saturn 5 rockets burned a mixture of fuel and liquid oxygen, which is an oxidizer (a substance that enables the fuel to burn without drawing in outside air).

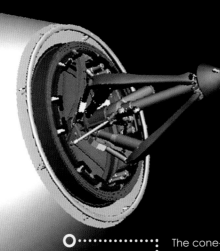

The cone-shaped command module was the crew's home during the flight to and from the Moon.

THE APOLLO SPACECRAFT

The Apollo spacecraft had three main sections. The astronauts rode in the command module. The service module carried oxygen and fuel, and had an engine. The lunar module was the lander. Only its top half (or ascent stage) took off from the Moon to rejoin the orbiting command module.

THE MOON RACE

1959 Russia sent Luna 1 towards the Moon; Luna 2 hit the Moon.

1960 Luna 3 flew around the Moon.

1964 US *Ranger 7* sent TV pictures of the Moon.

1966 Luna 9 landed on the Moon.

1966 *Surveyor 1* landed on the Moon. This was the first US unmanned landing.

1967 The first Apollo spacecraft caught fire during a ground test.

1968 The redesigned *Apollo 7* was tested in Earth, orbit.

1968 *Apollo 8* flew around the Moon 10 times.

March 1969 The crew of *Apollo 9* tested the lunar module and Moon-suit in Earth's orbit.

May 1969 *Apollo 10* flew to the Moon to test the landing procedure, but did not land.

July 1969 *Apollo 11* landed two astronauts on the surface of the Moon.

December 1972 *Apollo 17* was the final US Apollo Moon-mission.

The US space agency **NASA** directed thousands of people who worked on the Moon project. It was a huge team effort. Each Apollo crew wore its own mission badge on their spacesuits and they also chose their spacecraft's name.

THE EAGLE

• The *Apollo 11* lunar module was called Eagle.

• Eagle was 6.4 m (21 ft) high and weighed 13,000 kg (28,660 lb).

FAMOUS WORDS

• *Apollo 11* astronaut Neil Armstrong's first words on the Moon were:

"That's one small step for man, one giant leap for mankind."

• The *Apollo 17* astronauts left a plaque attached to their lander. It read:

"Here man completed his first exploration of the Moon. May the spirit of peace in which we came be reflected in the lives of all mankind."

MEN ON THE MOON

Six Moon landings were made by Apollo astronauts, from 1969 to 1972.

After a series of flights by Mercury and Gemini spacecraft in Earth's orbit, America sent the three-person Apollo spacecraft to the Moon. The event captured the world's imagination.

AMERICA'S CHALLENGE

President John F. Kennedy challenged Americans in 1961, saying his country should aim to land men on the Moon before 1970. The Apollo Program succeeded, with six landings (1969–72), and one near-disaster (*Apollo 13*), which ended happily when the damaged spacecraft flew safely home.

Apollo 11 astronaut Edwin Aldrin sets out an experiment package on the Moon. The photograph was taken by Neil Armstrong.

THE MOON BUGGY

The Lunar Rover or 'Moon buggy' was an electric car, tough enough to bump across the rocky, dusty Moon. It had a T-shaped control instead of a steering wheel, four-wheel drive, and a top speed of about 7 mph (11 km/hour).

Lunar Rover

THE MOON LANDINGS

Apollo 11 landed in the Moon's Sea of Tranquillity on 20 July, 1969. Neil Armstrong and Edwin 'Buzz' Aldrin walked on the Moon. Michael Collins stayed in the orbiting command module. In November 1969, *Apollo 12* landed in the Ocean of Storms. In 1970, *Apollo 14* landed in the Fra Mauro region. In 1971, *Apollo 15* astronauts drove the first Moon buggy. *Apollo 17* brought back 116 kg (256 lb) of Moon rock for scientific analysis.

Apollo 13 took off for the Moon in April 1970. After an explosion damaged the service module, astronauts James Lovell, Fred Haise and Jack Swigert nursed the spacecraft around the Moon and back to Earth, landing safely in the Pacific Ocean.

Apollo 13 after separation

Science experiments set up by the astronauts took power from solar panels. This *Apollo 11* science kit included a seismic experiment to look for signs of moonquakes.

The lunar module had a fragile foil skin and spider legs. It used two engines, one for descent and the other for leaving the Moon's surface.

DID YOU KNOW?

There is no air, rain or wind on the Moon, so nothing disturbs the footprints left by the astronauts. The Moon buggies stand where they were left.

Violent Sun-storms send out bursts of gas far into space. These bursts of radiation can upset electronic communications on Earth.

THE SUN AND PLANETS

Eight planets orbit the Sun and, with the Sun, make up the solar system.

The Sun is one of millions of stars in the universe. Even from almost 93 million miles (149.6 million km) away, the Sun appears to us as the largest object in the sky.

FAMILY OF PLANETS

In addition to the Sun and eight planets, the solar system also includes at least three dwarf planets, more than 130 moons or satellites of the planets, and many other smaller bodies including rock chunks called asteroids and icy, glowing comets. All this material is held in orbit by the massive gravity pull of their blazing parent-star, the Sun. The Sun is by far the biggest object in the solar system, with a volume about 1.3 million times greater than Earth's – which means all the planets would squash inside it!

Jupiter is the largest planet in the solar system. If Earth was the size of a grape, Jupiter would be the size of a grapefruit in comparison.

1 Mercury is the smallest planet. On average, it is 36 million miles (58 million km) distant from the Sun and is 3,031 miles (4,879 km) across. Mercury travels very quickly around the Sun, once every 88 Earth days.

2 Venus is the hottest planet, even though at an average distance of 67.2 million miles (108.2 million km), it's almost twice as distant from the Sun as Mercury. Venus is slightly smaller than Earth.

3 Earth is the third planet from the Sun, orbiting at a distance of almost 93 million miles (149.6 million km). It is the only planet known to support life. The Earth's diameter (distance across) at the Equator is 7,926 miles (12,756 km).

4 Mars orbits the Sun at a distance of 141.6 million miles (227.9 million km). About half the size of Earth, it has a diameter of 4,221 miles (6,794 km). Mars has ice caps and may once have had rivers of running water.

ROCK PLANETS AND GAS PLANETS

Closest to the Sun are four rock-planets: Mercury, Venus, Earth and Mars. They are solid spheres of rock surrounded by gas atmospheres. Much bigger are the four giant outer planets: Jupiter and Saturn (all gas) and Uranus and Neptune (gaseous with icy cores). Pluto, furthest from the Sun, was once said to be the ninth planet, but is now classified as a dwarf planet.

Between the planets is space, but it's not empty. Hurtling across it are countless comets and meteoroids (sand to boulder-sized bits of rock and ice).

SUNSPOTS

The Sun acts like a giant magnet. Changes in its magnetic field cause sunspots to appear. There can be as many as 100 of these cooler, darker patches at one time and the number of sunspots grows during an 11-year 'sunspot cycle'.

5 **Jupiter** is a vast mass of swirling gases – mostly helium and hydrogen – and has no solid surface. It is 483.6 million miles (778.3 million km) away from the Sun and is 88,846 miles (142,984 km) in diameter at the Equator.

6 **Saturn** is second only to Jupiter in size, measuring 74,897 miles (120,536 km) across. It orbits the Sun at a distance of 888.2 million miles (1,429.4 million km). Saturn has the most spectacular ring system in the solar system.

7 **Uranus** was discovered in 1781. Before then, only the five inner planets had been seen from Earth. Another gas planet, it is 1,783.9 million miles (2,870.9 million km) from the Sun and its diameter is 31,763 miles (51,118 km).

8 **Neptune** is four times larger than Earth. This far-distant gas giant was discovered in 1846. It orbits 2,798,6 million miles (4,504 million km) from the Sun, and measures 30,777 miles (49,532 km) in diameter.

Mars, the fourth planet from the Sun, takes much longer to orbit the Sun than Earth. This means it has longer years. A year on Mars lasts 687 Earth-days.

WHAT'S IN A NAME

• Mars is named after the Roman god of war. In ancient Greece, the same God was named Ares.

• The two moons of Mars are named Phobos ('fear') and Deimos ('panic'), after the horses that pulled Ares' war chariot.

PHYSICAL FEATURES

The biggest canyon on Mars is the Valles Marineris. At more than 2,490 miles (4,000 km) long, it could easily swallow America's Grand Canyon, which is 277 miles (446 km) long.

The biggest crater, Hellas Planitia, is about 1,100 miles (1,800 km) across. It was made when an asteroid, comet, or meteor, hit the surface of the planet.

The highest mountain on Mars, Olympus Mons, is about 16 miles (25 km) high. That's about three times taller than Mount Everest.

Mars

Mars, the red planet, is the most similar planet to Earth.

Mars is called the 'red planet' because of its red soil, which contains the chemical iron oxide – also known as rust.

LIFE ON MARS?

In the late 19th century, astronomers peering at Mars through telescopes thought they could see vegetation and canals, and wondered if there could be life on the red planet. However, when spacecraft started visiting Mars in the 1960s, they found no vegetation and no evidence of any life forms.

WATER

What has been discovered, though, is water ice – and where there is water, there is the potential for life. Mars has icecaps at the poles that get bigger in winter and melt in summer. It also has an ice sheet under the surface, thought to be left over from a time when the planet had a more humid climate, perhaps just several thousand years ago. Dry valleys and gullies also suggest that rivers once flowed across Mars.

COLD AND DRY

Today, the Martian climate is very cold and dry. In winter, the temperature can plunge to -125°C (-193°F) at the poles. In summer, at the equator, it can reach about 20°C (68°F). The atmosphere is mostly poisonous carbon dioxide gas.

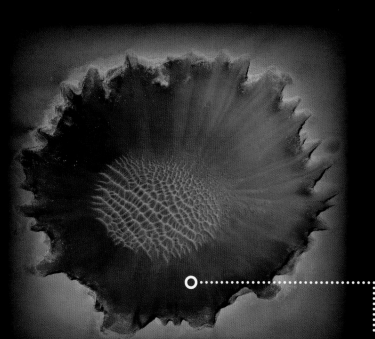

Victoria Crater was explored in 2006 by the Mars Exploration Rover Opportunity. A soccer stadium could fit inside its bowl.

LOW GRAVITY RED PLANET

Gravity on Mars is just 38% of Earth's. A person would feel only 62% of their normal weight on Mars. If they dropped a rock, it would fall to the ground more slowly than a rock on Earth.

Mars, with visible polar ice cap

On Mars, lots of fine dust in the atmosphere turns the sky pink and dust storms are common. Big storms can envelop the entire planet in dust-clouds. Hazy fogs are also common in the mornings.

Two Mars Exploration Rovers, Opportunity and Spirit, landed on Mars in 2004. Their panoramic cameras send back pictures that allow scientists to investigate past water activity on the planet.

Camera

Solar cells recharge the batteries that power the rovers' motors and science instruments. In winter, when there is less sunshine to recharge them, the rovers stop communicating with Earth.

Robot arm

VENUS AND MERCURY

Close to the Sun, these planets are too hot to welcome astronauts.

Mercury, the planet nearest the Sun, is about one-third the size of Earth. Venus is only slightly smaller than Earth, but is the hottest planet in the solar system, and is enveloped in poisonous acid-gas clouds.

GREENHOUSE PLANET

Venus has an atmosphere of carbon dioxide. Its thick gas clouds trap heat from the Sun, creating a 'greenhouse effect' on a huge scale. Temperatures reach 470°C (878°F), which is hot enough to melt some metals. Venus has no lakes or seas. The landscape is rocky and mostly flat, but there are volcanoes and mountain ranges up to 11,000 m (36,000 ft) high.

MORNING AND EVENING STAR

Although a planet and not a star, Venus is known as the 'morning' and 'evening' star. When it is moving towards Earth, we see it shining brightly in the sky in the early evening, and when it is moving away from Earth, we see it in the early morning.

Mercury is a ball of rock, rather like our Moon. It orbits the Sun on an oval-shaped path, so sometimes it is much nearer the Sun than at other times. Mercury has no moon, and only a very thin atmosphere. Experts think there may be water-ice in craters near the poles.

Venus comes closer to Earth than any other planet. The closest it comes is 23.7 million miles (38 million km). Like Mercury, Venus has no moon. Unlike the other planets, though, Venus spins clockwise. This means that on Venus, the Sun rises in the west, not in the east, as on Earth.

MAPPING VENUS

The Magellan spacecraft orbited Venus for four years (1990–94). It scanned the planet and, flying as close as 112 miles (180 km), mapped 98% of its surface. At the end of its mission, NASA sent it into Venus' atmosphere to study aerobraking techniques, knowing it would be destroyed.

Magellan mapped Venus in strips, using radar

DID YOU KNOW?

Magellan was the first planetary spacecraft to be launched by a Space Shuttle. The orbiter *Atlantis* carried it into space in its cargo bay.

MERCURY – THE SPRINTER

The Romans named Mercury after their swift-footed messenger god. This speedy planet orbits the Sun faster than any other planet, at about 30 mps (48 km/sec). It takes Mercury just 88 Earth-days to orbit the Sun (Earth takes 365 days). Mercury spins very slowly, however, turning once about its axis every 59 days (Earth takes about 24 hours). Only Venus spins more slowly. Mercury looks like our Moon. It has flat plains, cliffs and many craters made by meteoroids crashing into the surface. It is a hot, airless world, lit by the Sun – which looks nearly three times bigger in Mercury's sky than it does in ours.

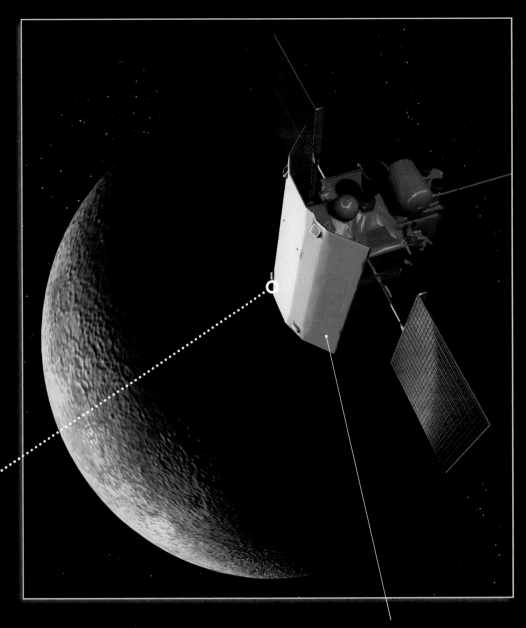

In 2004, NASA launched a probe called MESSENGER (short for MErcury Surface, Space ENvironment, GEochemistry and Ranging). Its mission is to study the planet with a variety of instruments.

Maat Mons is a volcanic peak on Venus, with lava flows visible. This image was taken from the Magellan spacecraft, as it orbited the planet.

A sunshade protects MESSENGER's instruments from the fierce heat of the Sun.

DID YOU KNOW?

Mercury gets very hot by day (450°C or 842°F), but very cold at night (-275°C or -463°F). With no oxygen and such extreme temperatures, nothing could live there.

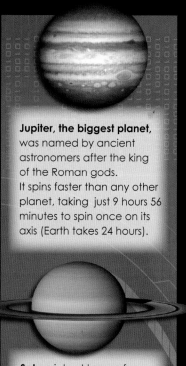

Jupiter, the biggest planet, was named by ancient astronomers after the king of the Roman gods.
It spins faster than any other planet, taking just 9 hours 56 minutes to spin once on its axis (Earth takes 24 hours).

Saturn is best known for the spectacular rings of ice particles that orbit the planet. There are seven major rings, each made up of numerous narrow ringlets, made of billions of pieces of ice.

Uranus is a world of blue-green methane gas clouds. Below them, possibly, are thicker cloud layers of liquid water and crystals of ammonia ice. The planet may have a rocky core.

Neptune takes about 165 Earth years to orbit the Sun once (Earth takes one year). It spins around its axis once in about 16 hours and 7 minutes.

THE GIANTS

The biggest planets in the solar system are largely made of gas and ice.

The four giants are the planets farthest from the Sun. Three of them – Jupiter, Saturn and Uranus – can be seen from Earth without a telescope; only Neptune is too far away. Jupiter is the biggest of the four giants and when viewed from Earth is brighter than most stars.

GAS AND WHIRLING STORMS

The giants are mostly whirling masses of liquid and gases, such as hydrogen and helium. Jupiter and Saturn are all gas – they don't have a solid core. Uranus and Neptune have icy interiors, though they are not solid ice. Gas clouds on the surface of the giants whirl and bubble in violent storms. The biggest storm is Jupiter's Great Red Spot, which looks like a vast hurricane and is up to three times as wide as Earth.

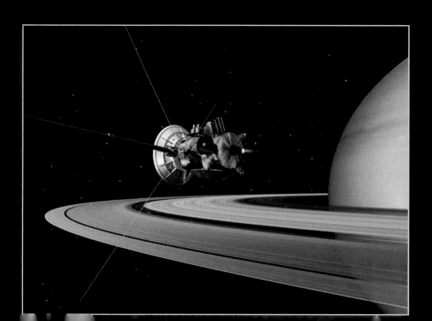

Jupiter's surface is made up of thick clouds arranged in belts, or zones.

The Cassini spacecraft arrived at Saturn in 2004, and continues to send back pictures of the planet and its rings. Cassini released the Huygens probe, which landed on Saturn's moon Titan in 2005.

Uranus was the first planet to be discovered with a telescope. William Herschel spotted it in 1781. It has at least 21 moons.

Cloud-covered Saturn has inner layers of ammonia, methane and water, with upper belts of hydrogen and helium, in places as thick as syrup.

Neptune has 11 known moons. Triton, the largest orbits in the opposite direction to that of Neptune, and may once have been a comet 'captured' by Neptune's gravity.

Great Red Spot

VISITING PROBES

Space probes that have visited the giant planets include Pioneer 11 (1979), Voyagers 1 and 2 in the 1980s and Cassini (1997–2004). These probes shed new light on the planets and their moons, revealing, for instance, that Saturn's rings are made up of thousands of bands, held in place by the gravity-pull of two tiny 'shepherd moons'.

SATURN'S MOONS

Saturn has 25 big moons, as well as more than 40 smaller ones. Here, the moon Dione is in the foreground, with Saturn behind. Tethys and Mimas are to the bottom right, Enceladus and Rhea are top left, and Titan, in its distant orbit, is seen top right.

Saturn and some of its moons

Asteroids, meteorites and comets

Numerous chunks of ice, rock and metal – much smaller than planets – orbit the Sun.

These chunks are asteroids, meteorites and comets. Studying them helps scientists to learn more about how the universe began.

ASTEROIDS

Asteroids are probably rocky material left over when the solar system formed. Most of them are in the asteroid belt between Mars and Jupiter. There are at least 750,000 large asteroids (more than 0.62 miles/1 km across), and there are millions of smaller ones. A few, such as Ceres, which is 580 miles (933 km) in diameter, are big enough for a spacecraft to land on.

METEOROIDS AND METEORITES

A bright streak of light flashing across the night sky (known as a 'shooting star') is a meteor. It's a small piece of rock, or iron, known as a meteoroid, which glows as it enters the atmosphere, leaving a fiery meteor trail. When Earth passes through streams, or clusters of small meteoroids, we may see a meteor shower in the sky. Most meteoroids burn up in Earth's atmosphere, but a few hit the ground and are called meteorites. The biggest one found so far landed in Namibia, southwest Africa and weighed about 60 tonnes. Thousands of smaller meteorites have been found by scientists in Antarctica.

Deep Impact was a spacecraft that sent a probe (about the size of a washing machine) to deliberately crash into the comet Tempel 1 in 2005. Deep Impact survived to photograph the event. The mission allowed scientists to discover more about what comets are made of.

Meteor Crater in Arizona, USA, was made by a meteorite measuring 50 m (164 ft) across. It hit Earth 50,000 years ago, leaving a crater 200 m (656 ft) deep.

Comet Tempel 1 was discovered by an astronomer named William Tempel in 1867. It orbits the Sun every five-and-a-half years.

Crater left by Deep Impact's probe, with gas and ice escaping

DID YOU KNOW?

The word 'comet' comes from the Greek word *kometes*, meaning long-haired. People thought they looked like hairy stars, because of their tail.

DID YOU KNOW?

Some asteroids contain water. This has led some scientists to think that asteroids gave our planet life-giving water and chemicals.

COMETS

Comet showing its tail

A comet is a 'dirty snowball' with a head of dust and ice, and a glowing 'tail' that streams across space. Every year, new comets leave the Oort Cloud – a belt of frozen comets at the edge of the solar system – and begin their journey around the Sun. All comets are left over from the formation of the solar system some 4.6 billion years ago.

SOLAR AND LUNAR ECLIPSES

An eclipse happens when the Sun, or Moon, is hidden, or is partly in shadow.

We see two types of eclipse from Earth – an eclipse of the Moon (lunar) and an eclipse of the Sun (solar).

A LUNAR ECLIPSE

About three times a year, the Moon's path in orbit takes it through the shadow cast by Earth, when Earth is between the Moon and the Sun. As the Moon passes through the shadow, it is eclipsed. When the Moon is completely in shadow, we see a total lunar eclipse. When it is in part-shadow, we see a partial eclipse.

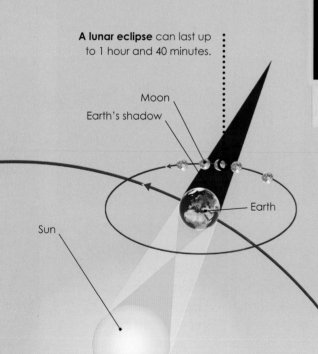

A lunar eclipse can last up to 1 hour and 40 minutes.

Moon

Earth's shadow

Earth

Sun

For a few seconds during a total solar eclipse, sunlight flashing between mountains on the Moon produces a dazzling 'diamond ring' effect.

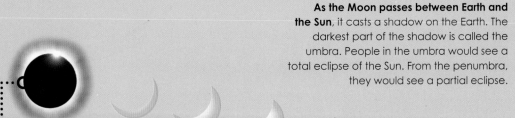

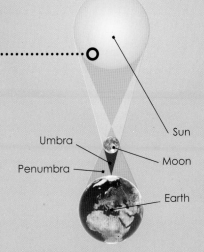

As the Moon passes between Earth and the Sun, it casts a shadow on the Earth. The darkest part of the shadow is called the umbra. People in the umbra would see a total eclipse of the Sun. From the penumbra, they would see a partial eclipse.

Sun

Umbra

Moon

Penumbra

Earth

During a solar eclipse, the Moon covers the Sun bit by bit until total eclipse, when a bright corona is seen around the Sun.

A SOLAR ECLIPSE

The Moon travels around the Earth. When it passes directly between the Earth and the Sun, it blocks out the Sun's light and the Moon's shadow sweeps across the Earth at over 1,864 mph (3,000 km/hr). This is a solar eclipse. A total eclipse happens when the Sun's disc is totally obscured by the Moon. A partial eclipse happens when the Moon only partly covers the Sun.

ECLIPSES HELP MEASURE LIGHT-SPEED

In 1675, Danish scientist Olaus Roemer was studying Jupiter. By measuring the eclipse-times of its biggest moons, he was able to work out how long light took to reach Earth. His calculation of light-speed proved to be 75% accurate.

Jupiter and some of its moons

In a lunar eclipse, the shadow of Earth moves across the Moon until it is completely in shadow (a total eclipse), when it appears coppery-red.

Optical telescopes (above) collect light. Most light-collecting telescopes today are reflectors that have mirrors to collect light. The first reflecting telescope was Sir Isaac Newton's (1671).

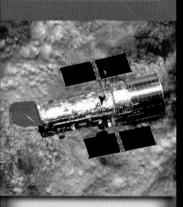

Hubble Space Telescope

The Hubble Space Telescope was launched in 1990. It orbits Earth, sending back incredible images of distant galaxies.

The spiral galaxy M100

Star-birth cloud, Eagle nebula

The Sombrero galaxy

Hubble is able to view objects millions of light-years from Earth, such as the M100 spiral galaxy. All stars are born from gas clouds such as the Eagle nebula.

STAR-GAZING

Stars have fascinated people since ancient times. Star-gazers were the first astronomers.

Modern astronomers use different kinds of telescopes to study the stars. Some telescopes collect light. Others, called radio telescopes, pick up other forms of radiation (rays), such as X-rays.

THE HISTORY OF ASTRONOMY

In ancient times, astronomers did not have telescopes. Using only their eyes, they named five of the eight planets and many stars. In the 1600s, telescopes were invented. The Italian Galileo Galilei was the first scientist to use a telescope to study the Moon and planets. Today, giant land-based telescopes, mostly on mountain-tops, and telescopes up in space itself, are helping astronomers to find out more and more about the stars.

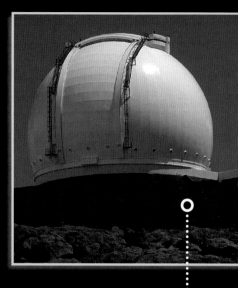

The Keck telescope is 4,200 m (13,780 ft) up a volcano in Hawaii. Being so high, it has clearer skies for star-gazing.

The Chandra X-ray Observatory was launched from a US Shuttle in 1999. It detects X-ray sources too faint to be picked up by radio telescopes on Earth, where the atmosphere absorbs most X-rays from space.

EUROPE'S HERSCHEL OBSERVATORY

Herschel, launched in 2009 by a European Ariane 5 rocket, is a space telescope with the largest single mirror yet put into space. The mirror measures 3.5 m (11.4 ft) across.

Herschel telescope

Herschel studies distant stars for clues about how the first galaxies formed and evolved.

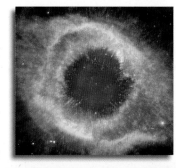

Star birth seen by Hershel

Radio telescopes have one (or many) large dish-antennas that collect faint radiation from the far reaches of space.

THE OUTER LIMITS

Radio astronomy was pioneered by Americans Karl Jansky and Grote Reber in the 1930s. Radio telescopes scan far-distant galaxies, searching for new evidence to explain how the universe began, some 13.7 billion years ago. Astronomy captured people's interest in the 1950s, thanks to big radio telescopes such as Jodrell Bank in England. The world's biggest is the VLA (Very Large Array) in New Mexico, USA, with 27 dishes, each measuring 25 m (82 ft) across.

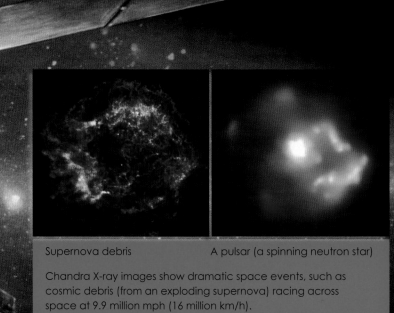

Supernova debris   A pulsar (a spinning neutron star)

Chandra X-ray images show dramatic space events, such as cosmic debris (from an exploding supernova) racing across space at 9.9 million mph (16 million km/h).

STARS IN SPACE

There are billions of stars growing and dying in the infinity of space.

A star is a ball of blazing hot gas. Stars are grouped in huge gatherings, called galaxies. Each galaxy has millions of stars. Our Sun is a middle-sized yellow star in the Milky Way galaxy.

LIFE AND DEATH OF A STAR

Stars are born in dust and gas clouds called nebulae. An old star may explode as a supernova. Before a small star dies, it may swell to a 'red giant', 100 times bigger than our Sun. Then it shrinks to a 'white dwarf', cools and fades.

DISTANT STAR-FACTORIES

In 2010 scientists discovered a galaxy so far away that its light has taken 10 billion years to reach us. This galaxy, known only as SMM J2135-0102, is 'spawning' new stars like our Sun all the time – perhaps as many as 250 new Suns every year!

A quasar is the brilliant outpouring of energy from a galaxy that has a supermassive black hole at its heart.

Black hole

Quasar

Gas and dust feeding quasar

Spiral galaxy

Hubble Space Telescope. This nebula was first spotted in 1844. In the middle is a spinning neutron star, the crushed core of an exploded star.

PULSARS AND NEUTRON STARS

The Crab Nebula is the remains of a supernova seen by astronomers in China in 1054. After a supernova, all that is left is a tiny, dense neutron star, spinning very rapidly and sending out radio waves that radio astronomers see as a pulsar. A pulsar is a neutron star that emits beams of radiation.

Galaxies come in various shapes – they may be spiral, oval, or irregular and are vast. It would take a spacecraft 100,000 years to cross the Milky Way galaxy.

The Milky Way, a spiral galaxy with an amazing 200,000 million stars.

A cartwheel galaxy – a small galaxy smashed through a bigger galaxy.

Circinus, a ring-spiral galaxy with 'starburst' rings and possibly a black hole.

Galaxies are often found in clusters of hundreds, or thousands, stretching away throughout the universe.

QUASARS

Quasars are intense energy sources, like super-bright stars, at the heart of some galaxies. They give off intense energy-radiation. One theory is that a quasar gets energy as a black hole sucks in matter from its galaxy. Quasars (short for 'quasi-stellar objects') are among the most distant objects detected in space.

A quasar not long after the Big Bang, the event that most scientists believe began the universe over 13 billion years ago. Exploding stars left ash-clouds of elements such as oxygen, iron and carbon – the building-blocks of new worlds.

The New Horizon probe was launched in 2006. Its target was to reach the mini-planet Pluto by 2015. On the way, it flew past Jupiter, taking close-up photographs of the giant planet and its moons.

New Horizon probe

Jupiter and its moon Io

Voyagers 1 and 2, two nearly identical probes, were launched in 1977. Their mission was to visit Jupiter (1979) and Saturn (1980/81) and their moons, with Voyager 2 going on to visit Uranus (1986) and Neptune (1989). Voyager 1 is now more than 10 billion miles (nearly 17 billion km) away from the Sun. Voyager 2 is passing through an interstellar cloud beyond the solar system. Both Voyagers still send data back to Earth each day.

SPACE PROBES

Space probes travel beyond Earth's-gravity to explore the planets and beyond.

To do this, a probe must reach escape-velocity, which is about 24,800 mph (40,000 km/h). The first spacecraft to escape Earth's gravity was the Russian probe, Luna 1, in 1959. Since then, probes have explored the planets and gone beyond the solar system.

EXPLORING THE PLANETS

All planetary probes carry their own power supplies, such as solar cells, batteries, or tiny nuclear reactors. Crammed on board are science instruments, computers, cameras, communications and small rockets or gas jets for steering changes.

Voyager 2 was the first probe to visit Uranus and Neptune. It's mission made use of the fortunate alignment of the planets Jupiter, Saturn, Uranus and Neptune, not due to happen again for another 176 years.

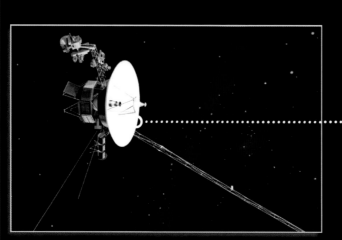

Voyager 2

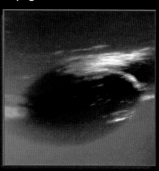

Neptune's Great Dark Spot

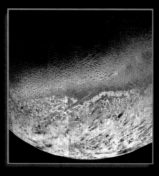

Triton

Amazing images of Neptune and its icy moon Triton were sent back by Voyager 2 in 1989. The Great Dark Spot on Neptune is a storm, like Jupiter's Great Red Spot.

FLYING THROUGH COMET DUST

The European Space Agency's Giotto probe had close encounters with two comets, Halley (1986) and Grigg-Skjellerup (1992). Giotto was damaged by a large dust particle as it flew close to Halley, but it continued to send back data.

CASSINI'S DISCOVERIES

Cassini was launched in 1997 and it finally reached Saturn in 2004. It revealed that Saturn has lightning flashes and that its moon Mimas has a huge crater – making it look like the Death Star in the *Star Wars* films.

During the Cassini mission's first four years, the Sun lit up Saturn's southern hemisphere. Now it is lighting up its northern hemisphere, allowing Cassini to observe sesonal changes on the planet.

Communications antenna

Computer

Cassini is studying Saturn and its many moons. It sent the small Huygens probe down to land on the moon Titan.

Main engine and spare

Arm holding a device to sense magnetic field

Huygens spacecraft

DID YOU KNOW?

Scientists measure planetary distances in astronomical units (AUs). One AU = the distance between Earth and the Sun, or 93 million miles (149.6 million km).

SPACE SHUTTLES

For more than 30 years, Shuttles have flown astronauts into space and back.

The US Space Shuttle is a space freight truck. It flies into Earth's orbit carrying a crew of astronauts, science experiments, satellites for launching and supplies for the International Space Station (ISS).

WINGS INTO SPACE

The Shuttle was the first spacecraft with wings. It takes off like a rocket, but lands like a plane. It has a big fuel tank for its rocket engines, plus two boosters that drop off when empty and parachute back to Earth, to be used again. At the end of each mission, the Shuttle re-enters Earth's atmosphere and glides down, landing on an airstrip.

THE SHUTTLE STORY

The first Shuttle, in 1981, was *Columbia*. *Challenger* blew up during launch in 1986, killing all 7 astronauts. In 2003, Columbia broke up during its return to Earth. All the crew died. Shuttles *Discovery*, *Atlantis* and *Endeavour* were scheduled for retirement by 2011.

Atlantis on the launch pad at Cape Canaveral. The huge fuel tank fixed to the spacecraft holds 2 million litres (440,000 gallons) of liquid oxygen/liquid hydrogen fuel.

SHUTTLE AT WORK

The Shuttle carries payloads in its large cargo bay, which measures 18.3 m (60 ft) long by 4.6 m (15 ft) wide. In 1990, it successfully launched the Hubble Space Telescope, shown here being deployed (released into space).

LAST OF ITS LINE?

The Shuttle was supposed to make spaceflight cheaper, because it was re-usable, but this did not really work out. It is now at the end of its working life and rockets are used for most satellite launches. America's plans for a new generation of shuttles for the next 20 years of spaceflight are uncertain.

The Shuttle ferries crew and equipment to the ISS. Here, the Shuttle approaches the space station with its cargo bay open and robot arm outstretched.

Landing the Shuttle, pilots say, is like "flying a brick". It glides in without engine power and uses a brake-parachute to slow the touchdown.

DID YOU KNOW?

In 1998 *Columbia* carried a science laboratory (Spacelab) in its cargo bay containing about 2,000 small animals, so they could be studied in space.

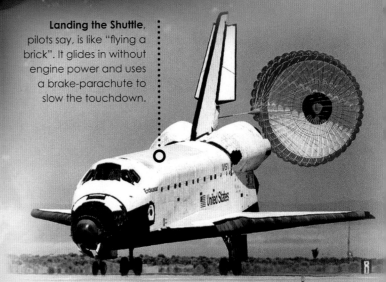

SPACE STATIONS

A space station is an orbiting science laboratory and living quarters.

The crew may live in the station for months at a time, conducting science experiments and photographing things not visible from Earth.

THE INTERNATIONAL SPACE STATION

The International Space Station (ISS) was constructed in stages from 1998 to 2010 by the United States, Russia, Japan, Canada, Brazil and eleven European countries. It was made from large sections, or modules, brought up from Earth separately by spacecraft and connected in space.

LIFE ON THE ISS

The ISS is big enough for six crew members. Fresh crews arrive in Shuttles. (After Shuttles are retired, they will be ferried by a three-person Russian spacecraft.) Some of the air and water they need is brought from Earth by supply craft, but some is made on the ISS. Crews eat food brought from Earth, and take regular exercise, because long periods of weightlessness weaken muscles.

After six years in space, Skylab re-entered Earth's atmosphere and burned up. Most of its debris fell into the sea, but some chunks of it landed in western Australia.

Solar panels make electrical power for the space station. They were fitted in December 2000 as the ISS took shape.

EXPERIMENTS

The ISS crew have been conducting experiments that may help planet Earth in the future. They are trying to find out, for example, whether they can grow plants faster in space, so that they can produce an alternative energy fuel, or biofuel, for use on Earth. Other experiments are looking into whether life on Mars may one day be possible.

Salyut 1, launched by the Soviet Union in 1971, was the first space station. Six Salyuts followed, with Salyut 7 (not used after 1986) in orbit until 1991. They proved people could spend months in space.

Skylab was an American space station launched in 1973. It used the spare third stage of a Saturn 5 rocket. Three crews visited Skylab, with the longest stay in space lasting 84 days.

Mir was launched by the Soviet Union in 1986 and was the first permanently occupied space station. It stayed in orbit until 2001, when its orbit got too low and it burned up.

Docking ports allow visiting spacecraft, such as the Shuttle, to lock on to the ISS. Crews transfer between craft through an airlock.

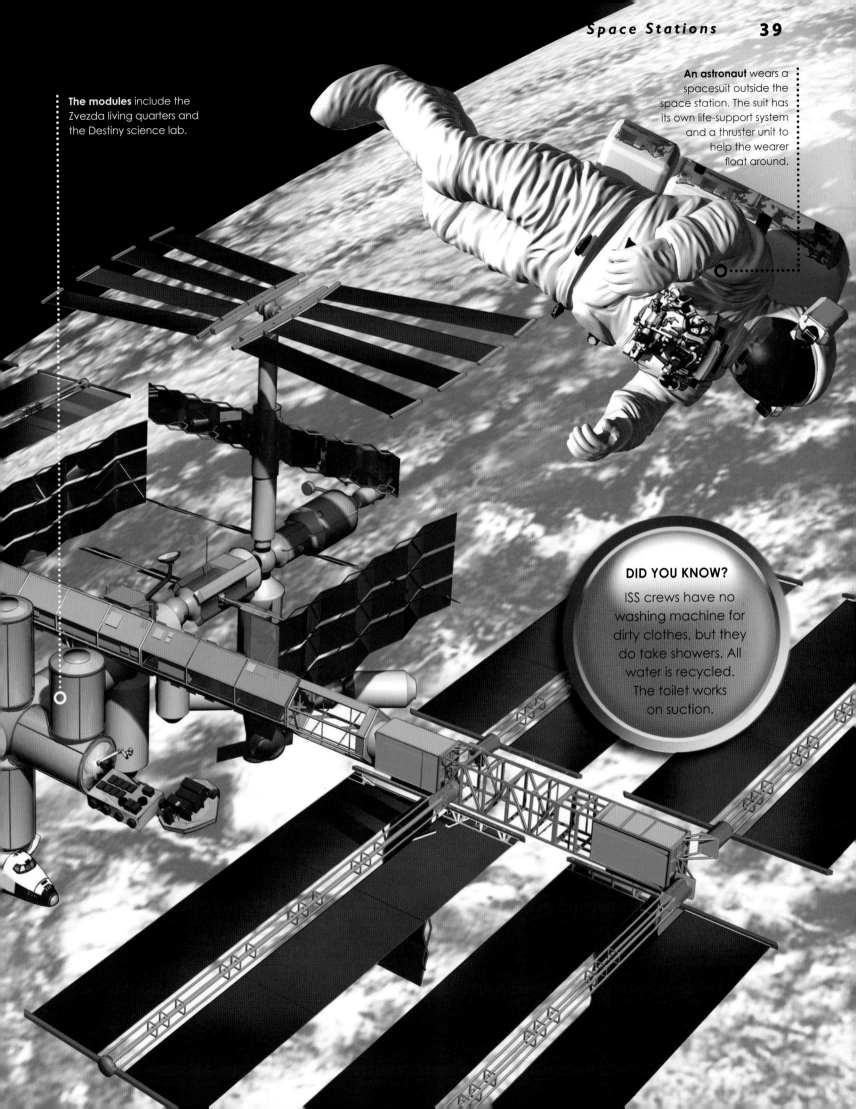

The modules include the Zvezda living quarters and the Destiny science lab.

An astronaut wears a spacesuit outside the space station. The suit has its own life-support system and a thruster unit to help the wearer float around.

DID YOU KNOW?

ISS crews have no washing machine for dirty clothes, but they do take showers. All water is recycled. The toilet works on suction.

LIFE IN SPACE

Living in zero gravity can be fun, but it requires extensive training and specialized equipment.

Without gravity (zero G), all objects, such as screwdrivers and screws, float around unless fixed down, and a person's body has no weight. Astronauts must brace themselves against something rigid to perform many tasks.

LIFE SUPPORT

Inside the Space Station, astronauts wear shorts and t-shirts. Outside, where temperatures are more than 120°C (248°F) in sunlight and -150°C (-238°F) in shadow, they must wear spacesuits. Orbital spacesuits, designed for floating, not Moon-walking, are made of layers of synthetic material, such as Teflon for protection from scrapes. A gold-coated helmet visor protects the astronaut's eyes from the dazzling sunlight and the inner head-cap has a built-in radio. Tanks in the backpack supply oxygen for breathing, while the astronaut is working outside the spacecraft.

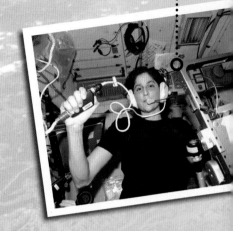

Astronaut Sunita Williams holds the record for the longest single spaceflight by a woman – 195 days, set in 2007.

The commander's station on the flight deck of Space Shuttle *Endeavour*, which docked with the ISS in 2010 to deliver the Tranquility module.

At mealtimes on the ISS, astronauts eat ready-meals and dry foods, to which they add water. Tasty meals help keep astronauts fit and in good spirits during a long mission.

A Russian Soyuz and a US Shuttle dock with the space station.

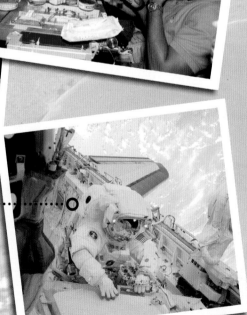

Construction of the ISS has taken over 10 years. Astronauts regularly check the space station, inside and out, and make any necessary repairs.

WOMEN IN SPACE

Women and men work together in space. In 2008, US astronaut Peggy Whitson was the first woman to command the ISS. On two missions, she has spent a record 377 days in space.

Peggy Whitson enjoying her spaceflight

SAFETY FIRST

Astronauts usually wear a safety line outside the spacecraft on EVA (Extra-Vehicular Activity). They can also lock their boots onto a robotic arm. One slip, or careless push, and an untethered astronaut could drift off into space. Tools can be lost that way, too. Spacesuits have a backup jetpack for getting back to the spacecraft in an emergency.

Columbus is a European-built science laboratory. Launched by a Shuttle in 2008, it is docked with the ISS, and has room for several on-going experiments.

DID YOU KNOW?
The ISS has an observatory module called Cupola, which has big windows so that the astronauts can enjoy the amazing views of Earth from space.

Upgrading the ISS in 2006, these two astronauts wore EVA spacesuits and jetpacks. They were installing a new supporting frame, or truss, brought up by Shuttle mission STS-116.

THE FUTURE

Space exploration in the 21st century is an exciting prospect.

Space costs, however, are now too huge for single nations to bear. The future lies in countries working together to make new projects happen.

Mars has excited scientists ever since Mariner 4 flew close to the red planet in 1965. Future 'scout' missions will orbit Mars, while the Mars Science Laboratory (2012) will fly itself down to a soft-landing.
This rover's mission is to find out whether Mars ever was, or is today, an environment able to support life.
The Sample Return Mission will collect Martian soil and bring it back to Earth for scientists to study.

Life on Mars remains a tantalizing possibility.
No life has been found so far, but future missions will examine likely places where evidence of past, or present life might exist, such as ice-filled gullies, or deep caves.

WORKING TOGETHER

To keep the ISS in service, new vehicles will be needed to replace the ageing Shuttle and Soyuz spacecraft. Since 2008, an unmanned Automated Transfer Vehicle has been supplying the ISS and there are plans for new manned vehicles to fly astronauts to and from the space station.

TRIPS TO MARS?

An astronaut-mission to Mars would take 18 months, and be both dangerous and difficult. However, Mars has resources, such as underground water-ice and minerals, that explorers could use. They could construct a Mars-base and use winged aircraft and roving vehicles to explore.

A future Mars base might look something like this. The base would provide shelter, air and water for the astronauts, who would have to grow plants to help feed themselves.

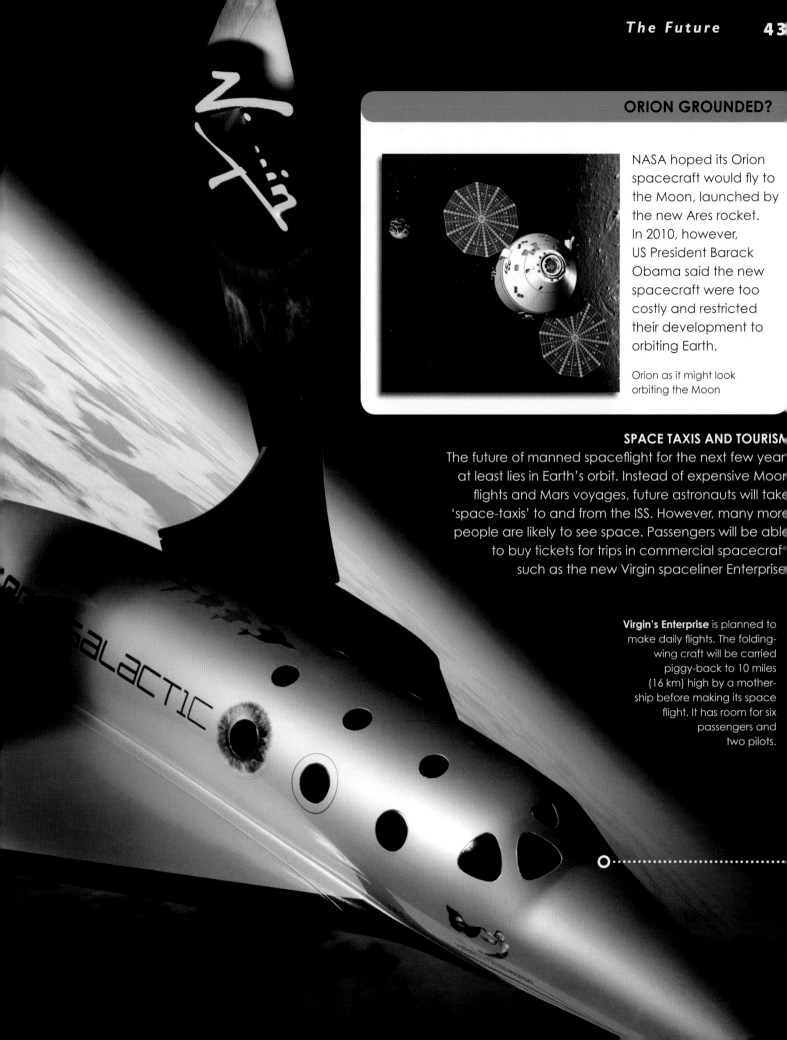

ORION GROUNDED?

NASA hoped its Orion spacecraft would fly to the Moon, launched by the new Ares rocket. In 2010, however, US President Barack Obama said the new spacecraft were too costly and restricted their development to orbiting Earth.

Orion as it might look orbiting the Moon

SPACE TAXIS AND TOURISM

The future of manned spaceflight for the next few years at least lies in Earth's orbit. Instead of expensive Moon flights and Mars voyages, future astronauts will take 'space-taxis' to and from the ISS. However, many more people are likely to see space. Passengers will be able to buy tickets for trips in commercial spacecraft such as the new Virgin spaceliner Enterprise.

Virgin's Enterprise is planned to make daily flights. The folding-wing craft will be carried piggy-back to 10 miles (16 km) high by a mothership before making its space flight. It has room for six passengers and two pilots.

GALACTIC

AMAZING FACTS

Nothing is bigger than space. Space has no limits and space-facts can be mind-boggling!

Space-speeds, space-distances and star-counts are incredible, yet millions of mysteries still await us. Here are just a few amazing facts about our space adventure so far.

Space starts 60 miles (100 km) above our heads, as we look up from Earth.

In the 1820s, Claudio Ruggieri, an Italian, experimented with sending mice up into space in a gunpowder rocket.

In ancient times, many people prayed to the Sun, believing it was a god.

The ISS orbits Earth once every 91.6 minutes at 17,162 mph (27,620 km/h).

The first woman to make a space-walk was Svetlana Savitskaya of Russia in 1984.

Space station crews enjoy eating tortillas. In the weightless environment, a tortilla is less likely to leave crumbs than a slice of bread!

FAST BURNER

In the first 2½ minutes of flight, a Saturn 5 rocket burned about 2 million litres (440,000 gallons) of fuel.

DID YOU KNOW?

Spacesuits have a built-in nappy system, in case the wearer needs to go to the toilet while wearing the suit!

WOMEN IN CHARGE

In October 2007, for the first time, two women were in control of both the ISS and the Shuttle. US astronaut Pamela McIlroy commanded the US Shuttle *Discovery* as it docked with the International Space Station, commanded by Peggy Whitson.

DID YOU KNOW?

In 1993, the Mars Observer spacecraft vanished from NASA's tracking screens three days before it was due to go into orbit around Mars.

So far, only 12 people have ever set foot on the surface of the Moon.

Because there is no wind or rain on the Moon, footprints left by the Apollo astronauts will still be there in thousands of years' time.

The longest time spent on the Moon's surface is 74 hours 59 minutes and 40 seconds. This record is held by Eugene Cernan and Harrison Schmitt of the Apollo 17 mission (1972).

The longest time anyone has been in space is 437.7 days. Cosmonaut Valeri Polyakov, in the Soviet space station Mir, orbited Earth about 7,075 times during this time (1994–95).

Astronauts in space breathe pure oxygen from their suit life-support system. On Earth, we breathe a mixture of nitrogen and oxygen.

Voyager 2 is now moving away from the solar system at roughly 29.2 million miles (470 million km) every year. Scientists hope to pick up signals from Voyager until its nuclear power sources finally give out.

Glossary

Aerobraking Slowing a spacecraft by flying it down gradually into the atmosphere of a planet or moon. Friction slows the craft without having to use precious fuel firing brake-rockets.

Airlock An airtight chamber, connecting two spacecraft.

Antenna A device, often dish-shaped, for receiving or transmitting electromagnetic waves, such as radio signals.

Astronaut A person trained to fly in space; the name means 'star-sailor' in ancient Greek.

Astronomy The study of space and the stars.

Atmosphere (Earth's) A protective blanket of gases forming the air surrounding Earth.

Axis An imaginary line through a body, such as a planet, around which the planet rotates (spins).

Ballistic Missile A long-range rocket weapon with an explosive warhead.

Black Hole An invisible yet incredibly strong gravity 'vacuum cleaner', that sucks up matter from everything around it in space.

Booster A solid-fuel chemical motor, used to launch a big rocket or spacecraft. The booster drops off when its fuel has been used up.

Constellation A group of stars that can appear to form a pattern, such as the shape of an animal.

Cosmonaut From the Greek for 'sailors of the universe', cosmonaut is the name used by Russians for their first astronauts.

Docking Joining one spacecraft to another in space.

ELV Stands for Expendable Launch Vehicle – a rocket used only once.

Escape-velocity The speed needed to escape from Earth's gravity into space – roughly 24,800 mph (40,000 km/hour).

EVA Stands for extra-vehicular activity, or 'space-walks', when astronauts leave a spacecraft to drift in space.

Galaxy A huge gathering of stars. There may be millions of stars in a single galaxy.

Gas One of the three states of matter; the other states are liquid and solid.

GPS Stands for Global Positioning System, the network of satellites for pinpointing location and helping ships, cars and planes navigate.

Gravity The attraction of objects to larger bodies, such as a planet or star. The gravity-pull of our Sun keeps the planets in orbit around it.

Interstellar cloud A cloud-like assortment of gas and space-dust inbetween galaxies.

Launch vehicle A rocket or spacecraft, such as the Shuttle, used to put satellites into orbit.

Light year Unit for measuring star-distances. Light travels at almost 186,000 miles per second (300,000 km/sec). In a year, light travels about 5.8 million million miles (9.46 million million km).

NASA Stands for the National Aeronautics and Space Administration in the United States, founded in 1958.

Nuclear reactor A power generator that uses fission (splitting an atom's nucleus) to produce energy.

Orbit The path (usually an ellipse, or oval) followed by a satellite or moon around a planet.

Orbit decay When a satellite's orbit gets too low, and it starts to burn, or break up as it meets the atmosphere around a planet.

Probe A robot spacecraft sent to explore the planets and outer space.

Radiation Giving off energy, as light, electricity or heat. Energy from stars travels as rays, such as X-rays.

Shepherd moons Small moons that orbit near the outer edges of a planet's rings. Their gravity appears to keep the rings in a neat shape.

Solar panels Light-collecting cells that convert sunlight into electricity.

Soyuz Russian spacecraft that carries astronauts to the ISS.

Suborbital A flight that enters space briefly, but does not make a complete orbit of Earth.

Index

PICTURE CREDITS
t = top, b = bottom, l = left, r = right, c = centre

NASA images are courtesy of nasaimages.org.

1l © Gary Joynes/ Beehive Illustration, 1r © NASA ; 2-3t
© NASA, ESA, and J.Hester (Arizona State University),
2-3b © NASA/JPL, 2-3b (small images, left to right) 1)
maps.google.com, 2) © NASA, 3) Satellite image by
GeoEye, 4) © chandra.nasa.gov/" >Chandra X-ray
Observatory, NASA, 5) © NASA, JPL, 6) © NASA, 7) ©
NASA, 8) © NASA, 9) © NASA/JPL-Caltech, 10) © NASA,
11) © NASA/JPL-Caltech and The Hubble Heritage
Team (STScI/AURA), 12) © NASA, 13) © NASA, 14) ©
Andrew Dunn, 15) © Courtesy NASA/JPL-Caltech, 16)
(no credit), 17) © Courtesy NSSDC, NASA; 4tl © NASA,
ESA and J. M. Apellániz (IAA, Spain), 4bl © Andrew
Dunn, 4-5b © NASA, 5 © NASA; 6l © Courtesy NASA,
6-7 (main) © Apollo 17 Crew, NASA; 7tl © Brunoil/
Dreamstime.com, 7br © NASA; 8cb © NASA, 8tr
© NASA; 9tr © Gary Joynes/ Beehive Illustration, 9
(main) © Stuart Jackson Carter; 10tl © NASA's Earth
Observatory, 10l © Courtesy NSSDC, NASA, 10-11 ©
ESA (European Space Agency) - AOES Medialab,
11cr © NASA, 11b (left to right) 1) © NASA's Earth
Observatory, 2) maps.google.com, 3) © Satellite
image by GeoEye; 12tl © The Russian Institute of
Radionavigation and Time, (http://www.rirt.ru), 12cl ©
El Christou, 12bl © NASA, 12 (background) © NASA, 12
(main) © NASA (NASA-HQ-GRIN) 13 tl © NASA, 13tr ©
NASA, 13 (main) © Gemini 4 Mission, NASA; 14tl © NASA
, 14-15 (main) © Celestia (rendering engine) and Chris
Campos, creator of the 3D model, www.shatters.net/
celestia,15tl © Brendan Howard/Shutterstock.com,
15tc © NASA, 15c © NASA, 15tr © NASA; 16tl © NASA,
16br (box) © 3drenderings/ Shutterstock.com, 16-17
(main) © NASA, 17tr © NASA; 18tl © NASA, 18-19 (main)
© Andreus/Dreamstime.com, 19br © John R Smith/
Shutterstock.com; 20tl © USGS, The Viking Project,
NASA, 20tr © Peter Baxter/Shutterstock.com, 20b ©
NASA/JPL-Caltech/University of Arizona, 20-21 © JPL,
NASA, 21b © Courtesy NASA/JPL-Caltech; 22tl © NASA,
22bl © NASA, 22-23b © NASA/JPL, 23tr © Johns Hopkins
University Applied Physics Laboratory; 24l (top to
bottom) 1) © NASA, 2) © NASA, 3) © NASA, 4) © NASA,
24cb © NASA, JPL, 24-25 (main) © NASA, 25br © NASA,
JPL; 26bl © Larry Bloom, 26-27 (main) © Pat Rawlings,
U. Md., JPL, NASA, 27b © Artshots/Shutterstock.
com; 28c © Oria/Shutterstock.com, 28-29b © Todd
Taulman/Shutterstock.com, 29cr © NASA, ESA, and E.
Karkoschka (University of Arizona); 30l (top to bottom)
1) © Pavelblag/Dreamstime.com, 2) © NASA, 3)
(left) © NASA, STScI, 4) (right) © NASA, ESA, STScI, J.
Hester and P. Scowen (Arizona State University), 5) ©
NASA/JPL-Caltech and The Hubble Heritage Team
(STScI/AURA), 30tr © NASA/JPL/Keck, 30-31 (main)
© Image courtesy of TRW/NASA, 31tl © ESA (Image
by AOES Medialab) with background by Hubble
Space Telescope, NASA/ ESA/ STScI, 31tr © 1971yes/
Dreamstime.com, 31c © ESA,ESA/Cluster, ESA/NASA
- SOHO/LASCO, 31br (left) © chandra.nasa.gov/"
>Chandra X-ray Observatory, NASA, 31br (right) ©
NASA/CXC; 32bl © NASA/JPL-Caltech, 32-33 (main) ©
NASA, ESA, and J.Hester (Arizona State University), 33bl
© European Space Agency and Wolfram Freudling
(Space Telescope-European Coordinating Facility/
European Southern Observatory, Germany), 33r (top
to bottom) 1) free resource, 2) © NASA/JPL-Caltech,
3) © NASA/JPL-Caltech/P. N. Appleton (SSC/Caltech),
4) © Andrew S. Wilson (U. Maryland) et al., WFPC2,
HST, NASA, 5) © NASA, ESA, Richard Ellis (Caltech) and
Jean-Paul Kneib (Observatoire Midi-Pyrenees, France),
Acknowledgment: NASA, A. Fruchter and the ERO
Team (STScI and ST-ECF); 34tl © NASA, 34cl © NASA,
34bl © NASA, Johns Hopkins U. APL, SWRI, 34c © NASA/
JPL, 34b (left) © NASA/JPL, 34b (right) © Voyager2,
NASA, 34-35 (main) © NASA, JPL, 35l © European
Space Agency; 36bl © NASA, 36-37 (main) © NASA,
37t © NASA, 37b © NASA; 38tr © NASA, 38-39 (main) ©
Norbert Sipos/Beehive Illustration; 40tr © NASA, 40cr ©
NASA, 40c © NASA, 40bl © NASA, 40bc © NASA, 40br ©
NASA, 41tl © ESA - D.Ducros, 41r © STS-116 Shuttle Crew
NASA; 42tl © USGS, Viking Project, NASA, 42bl © NASA,
42-43 (main) © Courtesy www.virgingalactic.com, 43tr
© NASA; 44bl © NASA, 44c © NASA, 44-45 (main) ©
NASA, 45bc © Gary Joynes/ Beehive Illustration, 45tr ©
NASA; 46-47 © NASA, 47r © STS-116 Shuttle Crew, NASA,
48 © NASA.